WITHDRAWN FROM STOCK

25p

0853 409 099 2 198 EC

Farm Animals

Dairy Cows

Ralph Whitlock

Illustrated by Anna Jupp

Farm Animals

Dairy Cows
Sheep
Poultry
Pigs

About the author
Ralph Whitlock has had many years' experience writing about natural history subjects. He is an acknowledged authority on wildlife and agriculture, and has travelled widely as a lecturer and broadcaster.

About the artist
Anna Jupp has worked as a freelance illustrator since obtaining an honours degree at Brighton Polytechnic. She is interested in biology and wildlife and enjoys combining these interests in natural history illustration.

First published in 1982 by
Wayland (Publishers) Ltd
61 Western Road, Hove
East Sussex BN3 1JD, England

© Copyright 1982 Wayland (Publishers) Ltd

second impression 1982
third impression 1984
fourth impression 1986

ISBN 0 85340 909 9

Phototypeset by
Direct Image, Hove, East Sussex
Printed in Italy by
G. Canale & C.S.p.A., Turin
Bound in the U.K. by
The Pitman Press, Bath.

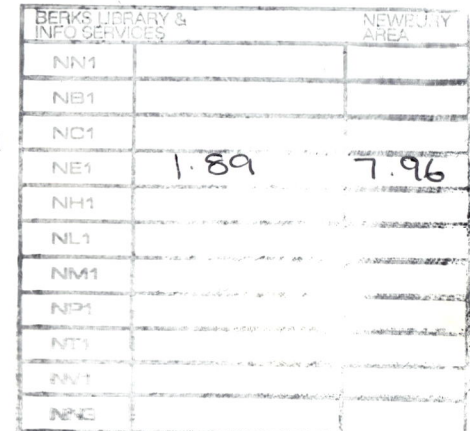

Contents

1	Milk—every day	4
2	Where does milk come from?	6
3	The cow makes milk	8
4	A calf is born	10
5	Weaning the calves	12
6	The cows go to be milked	14
7	In the milking parlour	16
8	The cows' milk is measured	18
9	The milk tanker arrives	20
10	The tanker goes to the dairy	22
11	The milk is packed	24
12	Different uses for milk	26
13	Butter and cheese	28
14	The calves grow up	30
	Glossary	32
	Index	33

Milk — every day

Most people start the day with breakfast. This family is eating cereal with milk and sugar. We need to eat many different foods for our bodies to work properly. Milk is one of the best foods we can have, because it contains amounts of all the things needed to keep us fit and healthy. There are *fats* and *carbohydrates* to give us energy and warmth. There is *protein* to help us grow and to resist illnesses. Milk is a rich source of *vitamins* and *minerals* too. The most important minerals are calcium, which strengthens our bones and teeth; iron, which keeps our blood healthy; and phosphorus, to help our brain cells develop.

This family of four uses about three pints of milk a day. Pouring milk on our cereal is only one way of using it. We may drink it just as it is, or add it to other drinks like tea and coffee, or maybe make it into a milkshake. We use it for cooking—custard, milk puddings, cakes, pancakes and many other dishes are all made with milk.

Milk looks like a pure liquid, but in fact it is made up of millions of tiny droplets of fat floating in a watery fluid. When milk is allowed to stand in a container for a few hours, many of these minute drops of fat rise to the top and form a layer of cream. The cream can be skimmed off and used to pour on puddings, decorate cakes or give a richer flavour to foods like soups and sauces. Cream can also be made into butter. Cheese, too, is made from milk. So in one way or another, we are likely to eat or drink milk many times during the day.

Where does milk come from?

All milk comes from female animals, who make it in their bodies to feed their babies with. This is the easiest way to feed babies during their first months of life. Dogs, cats, horses, mice, elephants and human beings all feed their babies with milk.

The milk that we buy comes from cows. In some countries people drink milk from other animals like sheep and goats, water buffaloes in India, yaks in Tibet and horses in Mongolia.

A cow will not make milk unless she has a calf. So, once a year (usually in winter) she will be mated with a bull and will become pregnant. When her calf is born in the spring, the mother will make milk to feed it. She will continue to produce milk for the next ten months.

For the first few days of its life, the newborn calf feeds on its mother's milk. Then the farmer teaches it to have other foods, so that he can take the milk that the mother is making to sell to us.

The most popular breed of dairy cow is the black and white Friesian, also called the Holstein. These cows produce large quantities of milk. Some other breeds of cow, such as the Jersey and Guernsey, do not give quite as much milk, but their milk is more creamy. Another common breed is the Ayrshire, which produces nearly as much milk as the Friesian.

The cow makes milk

This cow will soon give birth to the calf which is growing inside her. Once a year she is mated with a bull, and 280 days later her calf is born. She needs plenty of food to keep her healthy, to feed the unborn calf and also to produce milk.

Cows are *herbivorous*, which means they eat plants. In spring and summer, they can get nearly all the food they need from grass. A cow will eat as much as 95 kg (210 lb) of grass a day. She moves slowly across the field, tearing off mouthfuls of grass which she swallows without chewing. A cow has four stomachs, and two of these are used for storing the food she swallows. After a while the cow will sit down and begin to bring back balls of grass from these stomachs to chew. She may do this for several hours. It is called 'chewing the cud'. When the grass has been thoroughly chewed it passes into the other two stomachs for digestion. Some of the digested food goes to the cow's udder, where it is made into milk and stored.

In countries with an ideal climate, such as New Zealand, cows can live on fresh grass all the year round. In countries with a harsh winter, such as Britain, USA and Canada, much of the summer grass has to be preserved for winter food. Some grass is dried to make hay, and some is compressed when green to make silage. Cows are also fed on meal made from cereals such as wheat, barley, oats and maize. Sometimes they eat cabbages, beans, beet and other plants.

A calf is born

This calf was born only three hours ago. Its legs are still rather wobbly, but already it can stand quite well. It has to be able to stand so that it can reach its mother's udder, where the milk is stored. Once the calf has begun to feed, it soon grows strong and can run after its mother. In the wild cows live in herds, and have to keep close together for protection against attack by other animals. So calves must be able to follow the herd soon after birth.

The cow's udder has four teats which the calf sucks in turn. For the first few days after the calf is born, the mother's milk is especially rich in *colostrum*, which contains lots of protein, vitamins and antibodies which help the calf to build up resistance to disease. After about four weeks the colostrum runs out, but before then the calf is strong enough to manage without it.

This calf will never have any horns, because neither of its parents, nor its ancestors for many generations before them, had any. By carefully matching hornless parents, the farmer makes sure that none of his calves grows horns. He does this because cows with horns may hurt each other. Farmers who do not breed hornless calves specially can rub a chemical on the place where the horns would grow, which will prevent them from developing.

Weaning the calves

When it is a few days old, the calf can start to take other foods. The farmer teaches it to do this so that he can begin to take the mother's milk to sell to us. The calf has to learn to drink a milk mixture from a bucket, instead of sucking the milk from its mother. Sometimes, to show it what to do, the farmer holds his fingers in the liquid for the calf to suck. The liquid the calves drink is made up of skimmed milk and vegetable fats. Skimmed milk is ordinary milk with the cream taken off. Instead of each calf drinking milk from its own bucket, some farms have one big container fitted with a teat for each calf.

When the calves have finished their milk, all the buckets have to be carefully cleaned, to get rid of any germs. It is very important to do this, or the calves may become ill and even die.

The calf grows strong on its liquid diet for a few weeks, but later, like a human baby, it needs solid food. Every day the farmer gives it a few handfuls of little pellets of food, made from meal and vitamins. The calf also eats a little soft hay, which helps it to digest the other food.

What will happen to the calf? Male calves are usually fattened for meat. The females will eventually join the herd, give birth to calves themselves, and produce milk. A female calf is called a heifer until it has had two calves, then it is called a cow. Heifers usually give birth to their first calf when they are two to three years old.

The cows go to be milked

Now the cow is producing lots of milk but has no calf to feed. Twice a day she comes to the milking parlour to be milked. When the cows walk to the milking parlour, they always do so in the same order. If one of the cows tries to force her way to the front, the others push her with their heads, to keep her in her place.

Cows like their milking routine to be the same every day. In the milking parlour they always go to the same stall, in the same order. The cow's body is constantly making milk, which is stored in her udder. By milking time her udder is full and she is beginning to feel uncomfortable, so it is a relief for her to be milked. Dairy farmers like to milk their cows at regular intervals. Milking times are usually between five and seven in the morning and again in the evening.

If the cow were not milked the flow of milk would gradually dry up, but it would be very painful for the cow. If she is milked regularly, the milk flow continues for about 300 days. This is called the *lactation period*. The milk flow is at its peak a few weeks after the calf is born, gradually getting less and less until about two months before the next calf is due. Then the cow is 'dried off', to give her a rest before the next lactation period begins. 'Drying off' means gradually reducing the amount of milk taken from a cow, until she stops producing any. During her lactation period a cow will, if properly fed, give as much as 12,000 litres (24,000 pints) of milk.

In the milking parlour

In the milking parlour a milking machine is used to take the milk from the cow. The machine sucks the milk out of the teats, just like the calf does. When the cow enters the parlour she goes straight to her usual stall, where food is waiting for her. The dairyman works on a lower floor than the cows, so that his eyes are at about the same level as the cows' udders and he can work without stooping. He washes the cow's udder with warm water, dries it and then attaches a cluster of four cups, one to each teat. The cups are kept in position by a vacuum pump, which gently sucks out the milk once a second.

The milking parlour can be set out in many ways. In a traditional parlour, the cows stand in stalls side by side. In 'tandem' stalls the cows are placed one behind the other, so the dairyman has more room to work in. The most widely used type of parlour, especially for large herds, is the 'herringbone'. Here the stalls are set at an angle along two walls, and the cows all feed from the same trough. There are even rotary parlours, in which the stalls are mounted on a turntable and move round to allow the cows in and out. The stalls in rotary parlours can be arranged in tandem or in herringbone positions.

Another reason that the cow likes coming to the parlour to be milked is that she knows that there will be food waiting for her. The farmer carefully prepares a mixture of meal and vitamins, to make sure the cow has the best possible diet for producing milk.

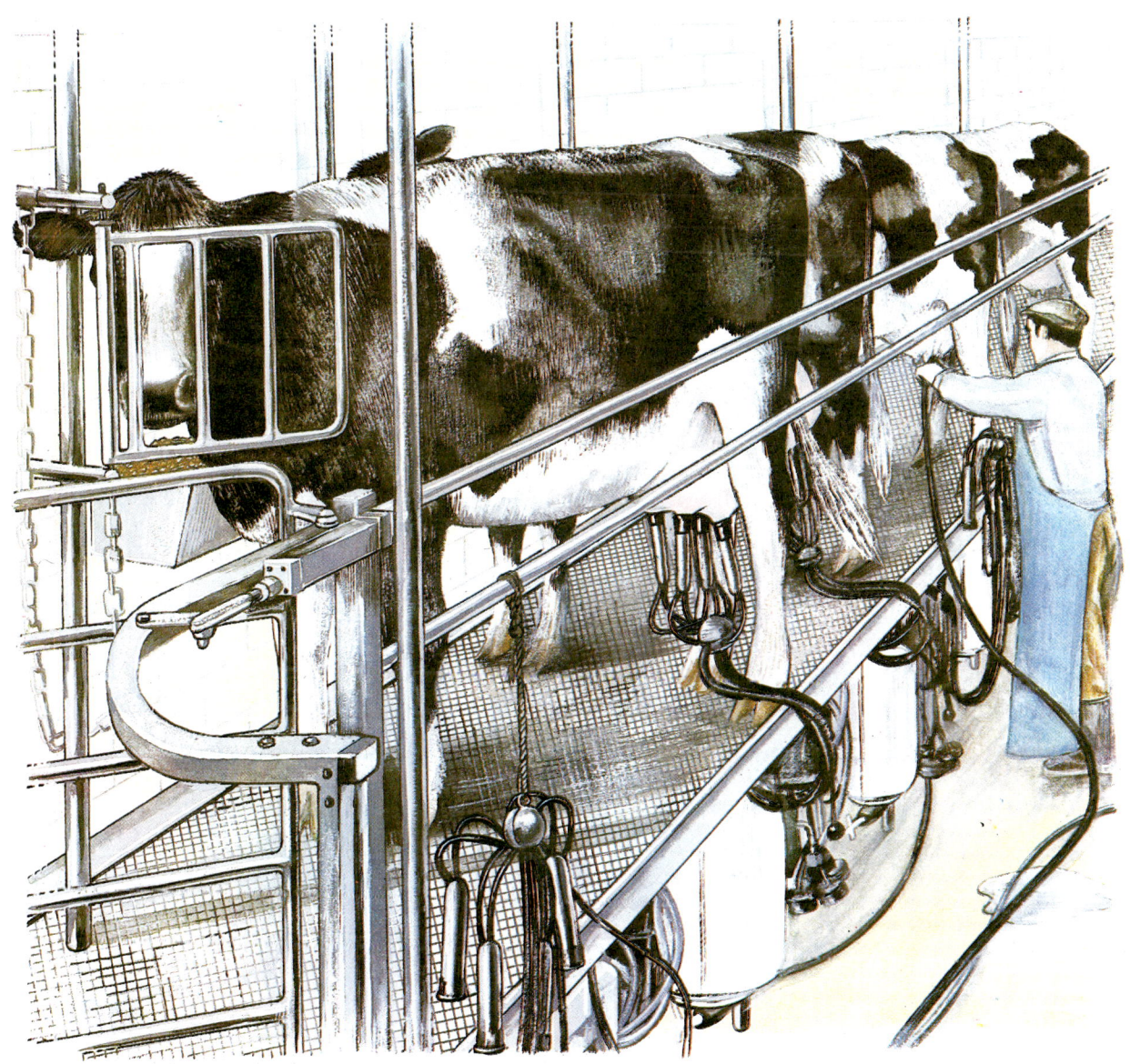

The cows' milk is measured

In the top picture you can see how the milk is collected. The bottom picture shows the dairyman measuring how much milk the cow has given.

The cows come for milking in batches. In this parlour the dairyman milks twelve cows at a time. It takes about ten minutes to milk a cow, though some give their milk more slowly than others. The milk from the cow's udder is taken along pipelines to a glass jar. The jar is marked to measure how much milk the cow produces. The dairyman enters the amount in his records, so that the farmer can work out whether his cows are getting enough to eat to produce as much milk as possible. If the cows are not getting enough to eat when they are grazing in the fields, they will not produce much milk. Then the farmer must give them extra food to eat at milking time.

When the cow has finished milking, the vacuum pumps will switch off automatically. From the glass recording jar the milk is pumped along pipes to a big glass-lined tank where it is rapidly cooled. If it is not cooled, milk may turn sour very quickly.

Everything in the milking parlour must be kept very clean, to stop germs getting in the milk. All the pipes, pumps and tanks are washed and sterilized after use. Disinfectant in hot water is pumped through the whole system, which is then thoroughly rinsed with hot water or steam. The dairyman wears a clean cap, overalls and gloves. After milking he washes down the parlour with plenty of clean water.

The milk tanker arrives

Every day a milk tanker arrives at the farm to collect the milk and take it to the dairy. Usually it comes in the morning, to collect the milk from the previous evening, as well as from the morning milking. The milk tanker is really a glass-lined tank on wheels. Like the farm storage tank, it is refrigerated, to stop the milk from turning sour. Most of the milk tankers which collect from the farms carry about 9,000 litres (nearly 2,000 gallons) of milk.

When the tanker driver arrives at the farm, his first job is to measure the amount of milk to be collected from the farm storage tank. He uses a measuring rod which he dips into the tank and reads off how far up the rod the milk reaches. This tells him how much milk is in the tank. It is important to measure this carefully, to make sure the farmer gets paid the right amount for his milk by the dairy.

When he has done this, the driver switches on the motor which operates the paddles under the lid of the tank. The paddles rotate and mix into the milk the cream which has settled on the top. This must be done, or the milk would be drawn off into the tanker and the cream left behind. Then the driver attaches a pipe to the bottom of the farm storage tank and the milk is pumped down the pipe into the milk tanker.

After every collection round, the tanker is cleaned. Warm water containing disinfectant is pumped through the pipe and the tanker, which are then rinsed several times.

The tanker goes to the dairy

At the dairy the milk is tested before the tanker is unloaded. Laboratory workers check a sample from the tanker, to make sure that the milk is as free from dirt and germs as possible, and that it contains the right amount of cream. Then it is pumped into huge storage tanks.

Next the milk is *pasteurized* to kill off harmful germs and make the milk keep fresh for longer. The milk is pumped through pipes to a heating chamber where it is heated to a temperature of 72°C or more for at least fifteen seconds. It is then cooled quickly. Some milk is given other kinds of treatment, which, besides making it safe to drink, have different effects on it.

Ultra heat treatment (known as UHT) is similar to pasteurization, but the milk is heated to a much higher temperature with steam. When the milk is packed in airtight containers it will keep for several months, even outside a refrigerator. It is known as 'long-life' milk. UHT milk is often exported to hot countries which have few dairy cows.

Homogenized milk goes through a process which breaks up the tiny droplets of fat so that they are spread evenly throughout the milk. So then no cream will form at the top of the bottle. Milk is homogenized by pumping pasteurized milk through very small holes under pressure. This breaks the droplets of fat down into even smaller droplets. This kind of milk is more easily digested than ordinary milk and has a smoother, more creamy taste.

The milk is packed

Milk has to be packed in small quantities for us to buy. After pasteurization or other heat treatment to make it safe to drink, the milk is packaged quickly. This is so that it can be as fresh as possible when it reaches the customer. Milk is sold in bottles and cartons.

In the dairy, a moving belt carries the cleaned empty bottles through a high-speed machine which fills each bottle with milk and puts a cap on it. This machine, which you can see in the picture, can fill and cap six hundred bottles a minute. Each bottle is sealed with a cap of metal foil. The colour of the cap shows which kind of milk is inside the bottle; pasteurized milk has a silver cap, pasteurized Jersey and Guernsey milk a gold cap, UHT milk a pink cap, and homogenized milk a red cap.

In many countries, milk is packed in cartons and sold in shops and supermarkets. Cartons are lighter than bottles to handle and transport, but they are thrown away after use, and that makes them more expensive. Bottles are used again and again, until they get lost or broken. When they are returned to the dairy they are thoroughly cleaned with detergent, disinfectant and hot and cold water.

Britain is one of the few countries which has a daily delivery of milk to the customer. More than 40,000 milkmen deliver bottles of milk to 18 million households every day. Usually the milkman comes before we are awake and leaves the bottles on the doorstep.

Different uses for milk

Not all milk is used in its natural state. The cream can be taken out of the milk, to be sold as cream or made into butter. The easiest way to get the cream out of the milk is to let the milk stand for about twenty-four hours. The droplets of fat will rise to the top and stick together to form the cream. This can then be skimmed off. In factories, cream is extracted by a machine called a cream separator, in which the milk whizzes round at a high speed. The milk, which is heavier, is forced out through holes, leaving the cream inside. Cream is pasteurized like milk to kill any germs. Some is also sterilized or frozen for long life.

Skimmed milk is the liquid left after the cream has been taken out of the milk. Although it is not a complete food like whole milk, it contains a lot of minerals and vitamins. Often the cream is replaced by cheap vegetable fats. When dried and powdered it is then often sold in shops and supermarkets. It is also used on farms, to feed calves and other animals. Farmers teach calves to drink skimmed milk so that the milk which the mothers are producing can be taken to sell to us. In this picture you can see the calves drinking skimmed milk from a special container, which has a teat for each calf to suck from. Skimmed milk powder is delivered to the farm in the big sacks you can see by the building. It is mixed with water.

Yoghurt is homogenized milk which has been heat-treated and cooled. A special culture is added which makes the milk ferment and taste rather acid. It is then cooled and packed. Yoghurt is good for us and is easy to digest.

Butter and cheese

Butter is made from cream. With regular shaking or turning, the droplets of fat in the cream start to stick together to form butter. The liquid which remains is called buttermilk. To make butter, cream is kept cool and stored overnight. It is then 'churned' to force the fat droplets to stick together into a solid mass of butter. This used to be done on farms, in churns or barrels which were turned by hand. After the butter formed, it was drained, washed, salted and rolled about until it could be patted into shape. Now all the processes are carried out by one machine. The buttermilk which is left contains many proteins and minerals. In some countries it is processed and made into a refreshing drink.

Cheese is made by adding rennet, a liquid which comes from a calf's stomach, to fresh milk. Rennet makes the milk clot and become solid. This is called the curd, and the remaining liquid is called the whey. The whey is drained off, and the curd is chopped up, heated to get rid of some whey, cut into blocks and left to drain. This picture shows the cheese being cut into blocks. It is then salted and put into a press which squeezes out any remaining whey and moulds the cheese into shape. The cheese is left to ripen or mature for many months. Whey is quite rich in protein and is usually dried for pig food. Dried whey powder is also used in modern processed foods.

The calves grow up

What has happened to the heifer calf which was taken from its mother when it was a week or so old? For six months she lived in a shed with other calves. At first she was taught to drink milk from a bucket instead of from her mother. Then she began to have solid food as well—a few handfuls of pellets of meal and a little hay. Gradually she was weaned to manage on less liquid and, instead, more pellets and much more hay. In the spring she went out to graze in the meadows, and there she stayed all the summer. She did not need any food other than grass.

The next winter she and the other growing heifers spent in another shed, where they were sheltered from cold, wet weather. They ate mostly hay and silage, but the farmer also gave them some turnips and kale, which he had grown specially for them. When she was two years old she was mated with a Friesian bull. And so, at the age of two years and nine months, she gave birth to a calf of her own.

Meanwhile, her mother had given birth to two more calves, one each year, with two months' rest between each. Cows can have as many as ten or twelve calves, but Friesian cows, which produce so much milk anyway, usually have no more than six or seven.

Glossary

ANTIBODY A substance produced by the body which helps to fight infection.

BULL The male of the cattle species.

CALF A young cow or bull.

CATTLE The collective name for cows, bulls and calves.

COW The name for the female of the cattle species, when she has had two calves.

DIGESTION The process by which food is dissolved in the stomach so that the body can get energy out of it.

DISINFECTANT A substance that destroys germs which can cause disease.

HEIFER The name given to a female calf until she has produced her second calf.

MEAL Animal food made from ground grain or pulses (beans, peas and other edible seeds).

PREGNANT When a female has a baby growing inside her.

SILAGE Green grass which has been cut and stored wet in a pit or silo. It is used to feed cattle in winter.

UDDER The large bag which hangs between the back legs of a cow, where the milk is made. It has four teats through which the milk can be drawn off.

VITAMINS Substances found in food which are essential for the good health of Man and animals.

WEANING Replacing the mother's milk by other nourishment.

Index

Bottles 24, 32
Breeds of cows 6
Butter 28
Calves 10, 12, 14, 26, 30
Cheese 28
Clean milk 22, 24
Cream 6, 26, 28
Dairy 22, 24
Feeding 8, 10, 12, 14, 26, 30, 32
Hay 8, 32
Milking 14, 16, 18, 32
Skimmed milk 26
Tanker 20, 22, 32
Udder 10, 16, 32